CAPTURED
BY THE
NORWEGIANS

CAP
BY THE

PUBLISHED BY J.W. EIDES F

ROBERT A. ROBINSON

TURED

NORWEGIANS

RLAG OF BERGEN · NORWAY

FOR BUDDY MY BROTHER — WHO WILL SERVE

AS MY SUPPORT ON THE UNCERTAIN PATH OF THE FUTURE,

AS HE WILL FOR ALL

WHO HAVE COME IN CONTACT WITH HIS COURAGE

First Edition

© Copyright, 1958, by J. W. Eides Forlag

Seven of the pictures included have won prizes in the *Popular Photography*
annual international photographic contest.

Made in Sweden and Norway
The photographs are reproduced in photogravure by
Nordisk Rotogravyr, Stockholm.

The letterpress is printed by J. W. Eides Boktrykkeri, Bergen,
and the binding is by Ed. B. Giertsen, Bergen.

Cover design and technical assistance in production by Reidar Johan Berle.

Photographed and Designed by
ROBERT A. ROBINSON

CAPTURED
BY THE NORWEGIANS

THIS BOOK has been compiled in a language which may be described but never spoken—its syllables must be understood through the medium of our eyes. Therefore, and because the pictures do not illustrate a definite plan or continuity, I have chosen not to employ a chronological text, nor has any attempt been made to interpret the contents of each picture in the light of the experiences encountered in my life, since I have contacted my subjects only through the limited perspective of the observer. Obviously, all I have been able to learn about them is insignificant compared with what they really are or might be. Similarly restricted, you as an observer are free to interpret the pictures in your own way.

Hundreds of photographs were taken as my curiosity led me on a somewhat arbitrary course of travel, my subjects appearing along the way. In the following pages I bring you some of those momentary encounters, hoping that you may derive some enjoyment from them, hoping too that you will see and understand the idiosyncrasies which do not set apart the Norwegian people from the rest of mankind.

The Norwegians as a people have, I feel, been sadly neglected by the camera in favour of more picturesque landscape photography. My purpose is thus to reveal them as something more than pretty blonde maidens kneeling in pastures filled with wild flowers and contented cattle. These charming features do exist, with their snow-capped mountains in the background, but, like Swiss chalets and American cowboys, they tend to obscure the real identity of a nation— in this case a people unusually free from social discrimination, which enables them to live as a family in spite of divergent local customs.

It would perhaps be unfair not to mention the Norwegian terrain, which is nothing short of incredible. There are places that seem as if they could not exist except in ethereal space—or perhaps I should use some other phrase to suit the infinite stretch of one's imagination. A traveller passing over high glacial plateaux will experience a feeling of crossing infinity, then, descending past gigantic masses of rock, will feel humility in its simplest form, coming finally upon a pastoral loveliness which will convince him still further of the insignificance of man.

You may gather that I have been impressed by the scenery into a state of romantic sentimentalism, and perhaps this is true, but I have tried to keep an open mind in my observations. In any event, Norway is one of Nature's greatest achievements. I mention it because I believe these natural elements are manifested in the Norwegian character. One rather admirable characteristic is a balance between modesty and aggressiveness.

In conclusion I should like to express my personal gratitude for the friendly welcome Norwegians have given me during the many months I have analysed them through my camera. Some day I should like to record them again in a yet more intimate way, and perhaps I shall—for the title of this book is an exact interpretation of my feelings.

Robert A. Robinson

Shafts of sunlight give birth to a spring morning

And yet, though we try, we never recapture
the world of childhood

. . . Thus he will carve himself in stone,
that he may remain suspended in celestial space
And when this stone of his endeavour descends to dust,
reality will have passed him by
For man is but one grain of sand in the hourglass of time . . .

Alfred Jens
FETEVAREFORRETNING
Telefon 12041
SMØR
OST
Klöversmör
Bondesmör
Gammelost
Gjetost
Sirup i Boxer
Appelsin-Marmelade
Tyttebær
Jordbær
God-Kaffe
SMØR
OST
EGG
VILT
HERMETI

*Man's curiosity may stem from his ability to create
an abundance of curiosities*

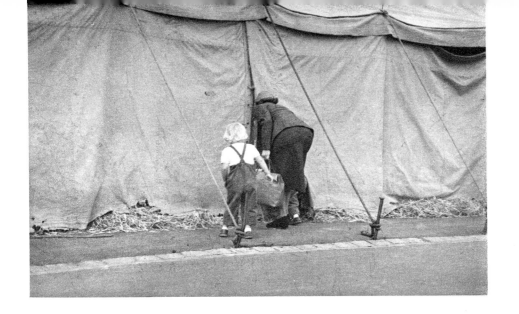

This night of utter stillness . . . startling in its silence

*Life steers an unalterable course amid
the clutter of human inventiveness*

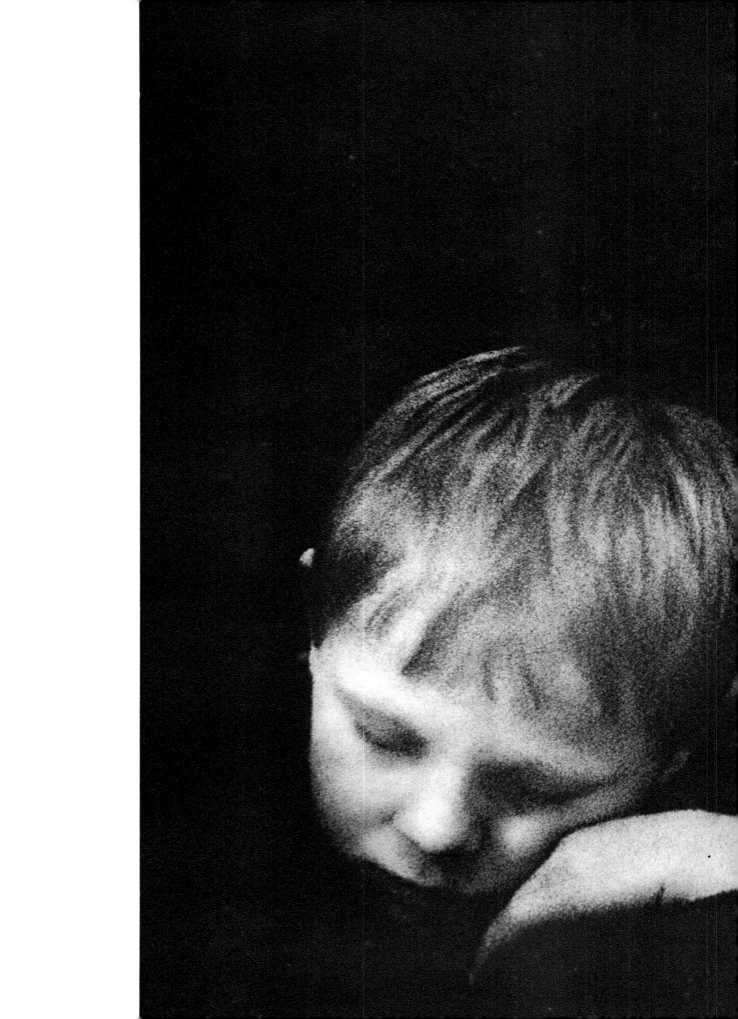

Each day brings forth a new necessity . . . a new challenge

The Pied Pipe and Pipers

If a smile
could remain . . .

*Each May 17TH
the nation
is reborn in spirit*

People will gather here as one

Changing seasons

Let our needs set the pace . . .

. . . and changes will come in the order of things

Throughout the land
bonfires spring forth,
adding their glow
to the twilight hour of
Midsummer Night

*Vast shoals of codfish hidden in the depths of the
North Sea proved to be a phenomenal discovery . . .
Thus grew up an industry and hardy fisher-folk
gathered on the scene amid the islands of Lofoten*

To each in his leisure his own delight

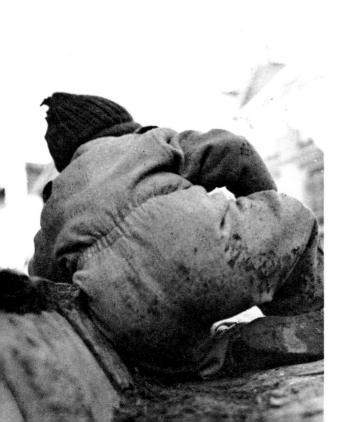

A lifetime of desires
A lifetime of dreams

Evil is of the mind alone
Kindness—a way of the heart

We gather in humble tribute

*Man
shapes
his
environment . . .*

My home is my castle

Varied are the interests of children

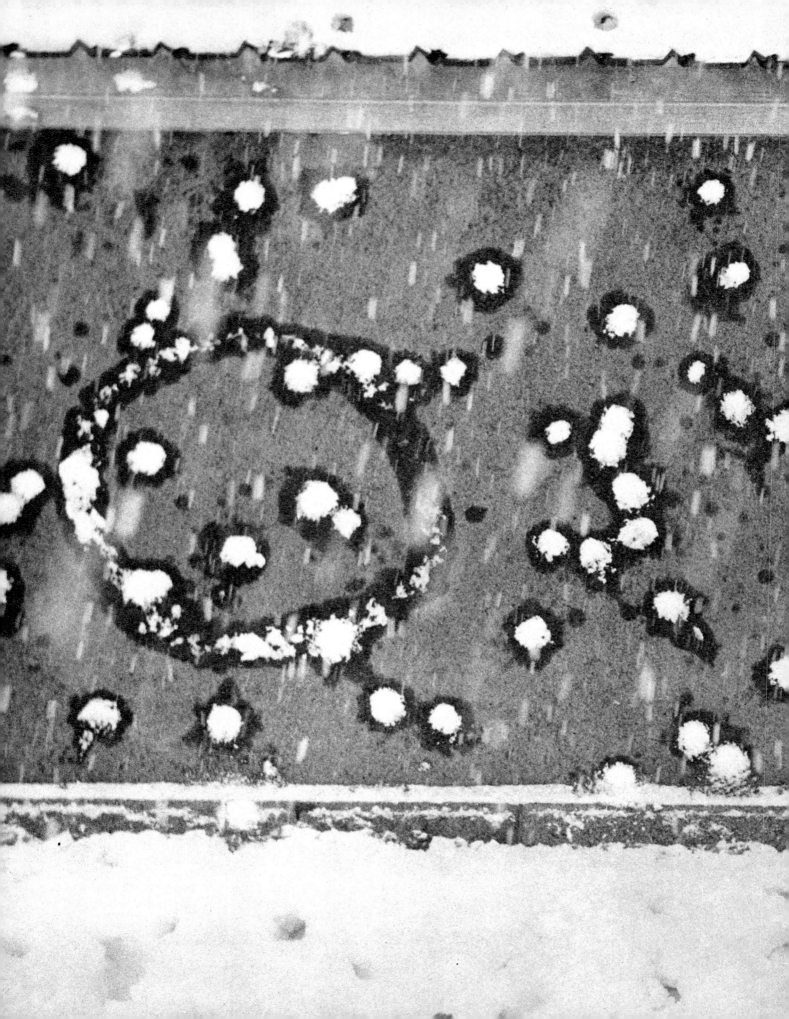

Vahls gate

The essence of summer
is manifested
in the triumph of winter . . .

. . . its first subtle scent
  reborn on the broad shoulders of a spring breeze

And all that summer is
we will absorb through our senses . . .

. . . and respond to its stimulating presence

We take leisure in summer's warmth
And when we have drunk our fill,
Our thoughts embrace the winter past
And we remember apart from its brittle cold,
Longing for the coming change

The sea—gateway to dreams of adventure and distant lands

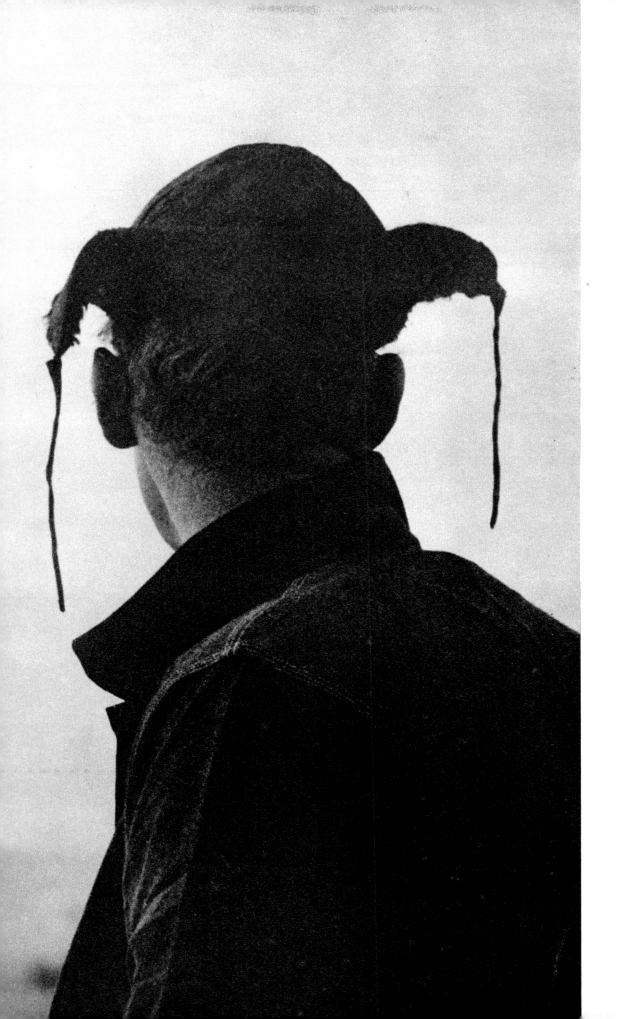

*Silver
harvest
of the sea*

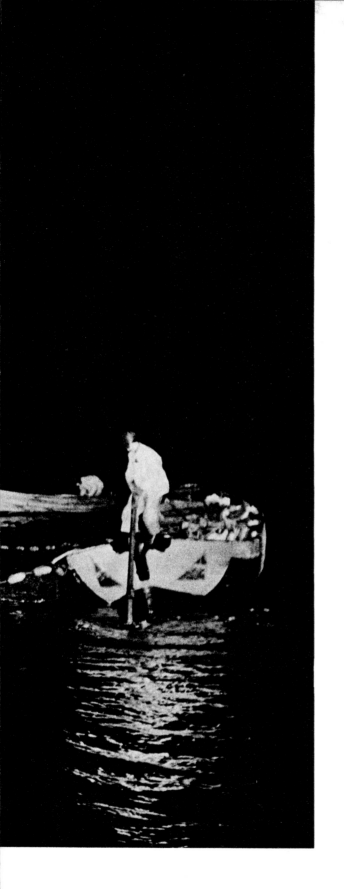